All the Holes Line Up

Poems and Translations
by
Zackary Sholem Berger

The Jewish Poetry Project
Ben Yehuda Press

Teaneck, New Jersey

Other Books of Poetry and Translations by Zackary Sholem Berger

Di Kats der Payats (The Cat in the Hat in Yiddish), Twenty-Fourth Street Books, 2003
Curious George in Yiddish, George Der Naygeriker, Yiddish House LLC, 2005
Eyn Fish Tsvey Fish Royter Fish Bloyer Fish: One Fish Two Fish Red Fish Blue Fish in Yiddish, Yiddish House LLC, 2008
Not in the Same Breath: A Yiddish & English Book of Poetry, Yiddish House LLC, 2011
One Nation Taken Out of Another, Apprentice House, 2014
Vi Lebt Zikh Dortn (What It's Like), poems in Yiddish and Hebrew, self-published, 2018
Collected Prose of Avrom Sutzkever (forthcoming)

Other Books Including Translations by Zackary Sholem Berger

Sudden Rain (Yiddish poetry), Yisroel-bukh, 2003
The Ecco Anthology of International Poetry, Ecco, 2010

The Jewish Poetry Project — jPoetry.us

1. *From the Coffee House of Jewish Dreamers* by Isidore Century
2. *The House at the Center of the World* by Abe Mezrich
3. *we who desire* by Sue Swartz
4. *Open My Lips* by Rachel Barenblat
5. *Words for Blessing the World* by Herbert Levine
6. *Shiva Moon* by Maxine Silverman
7. *is* by Yaakov Moshe
8. *Texts to the Holy* by Rachel Barenblat
9. *The Sabbath Bee* by Wilhelmina Gottschalk
10. *All the Holes Line Up* by Zackary Sholem Berger

*This book made possible
through the generosity of*
Ruthie Levi

ALL THE HOLES LINE UP: POEMS AND TRANSLATIONS Copyright © 2019 by Zackary Sholem Berger. All rights reserved. No part of this book may be used or reproduced in any manner whatsoever without written permission except in the case of brief quotations embodied in critical articles and reviews.

Published by Ben Yehuda Press
122 Ayers Court #1B / Teaneck, NJ 07666
http://www.BenYehudaPress.com
ISBN13 978-1-934730-73-7

Acknowledgments

Grateful acknowledgment is provided to the journals in which the following poems appeared previously.

"Everything Has a Hole in It," "Anatomy," "What It's Like," "I wake up with a craving for the whole damn diamond" – *The Legendary*

"Irregularity" – *Antiphon*

"City, this Baltimore." – *Jersey Devil Press*

"I embrace certain certainties," "I have never been lost in the city I moved to (City, 4)" "I have never caught on fire." "1975 [Explain it? Explain it how?]" "Some Guys" – *The Potomac Journal*

Poems in "Sanctity of Others" are exhibited at the Chapel in Morgan State University with photographs by Jeremy Kargon.

From Diary Poems ("Of course, your ladder's inside you. In-you is your ladder.") – *Blue Lyra Review*

"Herring Barrels", "My Pedigree" – *Eleven Eleven Literary Journal*

"I Prefer", "I Won't Ask" – *Outlook: Canada's Progressive Jewish Magazine*

"The Shadow" – *The Manhattanville Review*

21 20 19 / 5 4 3 2 1   20190114

All the Holes Line Up

Table of Contents

Alef. Organs and Cities	1
Bet. The Sanctity of Others	21
Gimel. Scrabbling for Shards	45
Daled. The Ladder Inside You –Translations	53
Heih. Willing a Rhyme – Closing	73
About the Translated Poets	80
Glossary	81
About the Author	82

Alef. Organs and Cities

Everything has a Hole in It

Everything has a hole in it
and all the holes line up
a telescope of defect
a tube of not-enough
to see right through to error
or what might come to pass
You try to catch the football
and whump right on your ass
remember that you never
should play a sport at all.
Passivity's your call.
This should have been foreseen:
mene, tekel, ufarsin.
So how can we repair?
What thoughts can we select
Already on the stair
Away from the repast
Full of insult and eclairs?
There is a lining up of holes.
There is a defect-rich alignment.
This they did not teach in school.
You give yourself this one assignment.

Mindful Design

Designed into my integument
the mirror
of some distant target

I am the sum
of my disintegrations

Caveat

No special knowledge is available.
Cortical curlicues
code the spiky datum
but strangle, or let slip,
what we have been chasing
or fleeing:
gnawing desire. Self-redesign
to capture what they can't.

Anatomy

In the membrane of my heart
curls a cardiac worm,
uncorking bloodflow's spurt
as current squirms.

"That's not how these things work!
There IS no 'cardiac worm'!"
But my muscle is verrucous.
And sensations: vermiform.

Irregularity

Knitting a serenade
from vibrations, the fiddle
thickens the air.

By the metal door
noise squats and waits
as it's replaced, curses all

intervals, symmetry,
clockwork of waves,
echoing caves: prefers

nervous saccade,
the well child
gasping suddenly, falling ill.

What it wants

In every temporary state
a terror makes its frantic way
out of the clock, hand over hand
into the mist subcorticate.

Stability is what the what-
ever implanted deep upstairs
thinks it wants. Or so we're told.
Evolution-psych, all that.

Modernity though is not enough
to decipher what we know is quick
panic, rising in our nodes
making our sinus rhythm rough.

Transience is our innermost
and embodiment the shape it takes.
Our fear is that we know too well.
We cannot last more than we must.

City, this Baltimore.

Nearer the campus
bird houses ride
three to a tree.

Dogs raise eyebrows
at stroller's cargo:
baby, toes dangling.
Off to a coffee.

Shot on a block
not far from here:
Our black neighbors.
I doctor some later.

City is shuddering
Blood on its buses,
its work and play shirts.
Crying in sleep.

Poe did not mean
The tale of these hearts.
Infarcted bodies
Flame in the sun.

Belief is concrete.
Something yet
To build, pay for.
To make, love for.

What It's Like

Myths bloom among mistakes.
A voyage of secrets:
along the routes of truth
you hear real screams.

Put down your pencil. People are dying
on the artists' street.
What's the point of rhyme
when your body doesn't know what's worse:

instant fire, or aimlessness
in endless hallways.
The poetic license expires.

Put down your pencil. You manage
instant sympathy.
You feel in your entrails
the hand of annihilation.

A missile eliminates
A bomb shatters you.

You are now expert in possible demises
The end of a straw-packed trunk of dreams

What's life like
in death's developments?

I embrace certain certainties,

unsure which to love.
Leaning on my horn at Stop &
Go, neurons hanging fire,
legs and guts awaiting
cortical orders.

Peace and Health throw colored veils
over shards. Together
we are seeking the most least truth,

That well which least contaminates our ends,
the wale which we will, ending,
wind upon.

Sean

My high school friend was tall and pale, with long
    fingers.
After exploration, he went to medical school,
Then family-practice residency in Wyoming,
Learning to judge a bullet's caliber
From its particular clang in a bedpan.
In Kentucky, Arizona, California, he was a locum
Then treated alcoholic schizophrenics in Louisvlle.

My friend Jon called me: Julie had found him down
In their bathroom. Not yet aged 40. I wondered what
    he died of —
No, what was the diagnosis. CVA. PE. MI.
He might never had known. And no autopsy:
No one would. I didn't go to the funeral
But called his mother. Awkward. Praised his healing.
"But you do that too," she pointed out, confused or
    annoyed,
And I realized that I do indeed.
Emulating him as I did in high school, my friend,
    now gone,
Kentucky doctor.

Travelogue: Intermittent

Box of scraps and fragments
Tentatively set on wheels
Caroming down the crowded street:
Watch where the fu—-

Suddenly over the hills, an effulgence
Where top earth and bottom sky meet.
Set back on my heels,
Disoriented in my integument

I let my contraption crash at the foothill.
Wrestling lostness into the compass
A protective seal and shield
Becomes the day's name and age.

City, 2

Voices drift down my block.
We should leave the doors unlocked

Though we don't. Greetings to new neighbors.
Who practices what's averred?

Like a scrap the truth is scrit on
This bench's edgy to sit on.

Still Life, With Movement

No special creation can be cited
Because physics has unrolled itself
Like a holy scroll dropped onto a floor.

You walk into a room and your body comes with.
Both halves you have taken time to assemble.
A ceiling lamp shines through dresses in the closet.

Transformations are the hobgoblin.
At the wall some coins have been left
Scattered. The owner given up hope.

The Scythe

Nothing can be promised
Since prediction is a net
To catch the rain
Woven out of rain

Nothing will fail
Since all is here
You and I and warm
Words between us

Building a world
Insufficient, laugh
Ably small
All we have

Denying death
Nothing is denied
I find a scythe
Cut babke with it

City, 3

Is the world collapsing?
Perhaps sing
A song about your nose
That sticks out and everyone knows.

Is the city dying?
Maybe try
Blowing up balloons and popping them.
Historicizing bullets to stop them.

Are you in need of love?
What's the need you speak of?
Cactuses extend their arms.
Electrons' negativity has charm.

46

Love takes its time
to cast its blossoms
like birthday flowers
and spread its fragrant
melting petals
among dropped Cheerios
and broken crayons.
Arrived at, not arranged.
Loved, not kept.
Faded, deathless.

I have never been lost in the city I moved to (City, 4)

but when I visit my birthcity the cows low my name
soft and tenderly, so I go to them in the fields
and listen to the delivery trucks bumble by.
Every man- and pothole sings its song.
I visit people I knew in school, the beer
tastes like dandelions must, the sports teams
lose charmingly, there is a famous bridge
and horrible suicides. I went to the hospital
the last time I was there.
My leg was broken and I got an infection.

In the city I moved to, the butterflies
know where my girlfriend's apartment is
and show me the way when I arrive
at the bus station. She is expert in French.
We have never spoken to each other
nor kissed, but bake fiendishly
and extravagantly
till the entire hallway is filled with strangers
stretching out their hands for baguette.

I have never caught on fire.

I am more than the sum of my fevers, and as my sweat rises on me at night, I look at the moon and feel my years folding themselves into paper airplanes, flying under an unused piano in the foyer.

The dogs here, the luggage there, the porch swept: sunflowers bending their clownish heads in prayer, forgiveness, or capitulation.

There is no sitting around while the clock's digits flutter at night. There is only a leaf that passes by the window, the wrong slip of tree at the wrong time.

Perhaps around this area there is an invisible circular outline. Or these columns rising after every step of mine are where I have trampled some barely registered sign carved into the ground.

Please sit down next to me and record your impressions of this scene as well. Together, we will build a rickety contraption that will assume its own burden, lumbering into the sunset without a glance behind.

Bet. The Sanctity of Others

Ten Commandments are Not Enough

Six hundred thir
teen don't even
saturate
the terrifying space
of choice.
We can always do
something else?
Help me, compromiser
keep my
inadequate choices
at bay
not whimpering on chains
not weeping in twilight
but crouching
for a morsel

Sultan Ahmed Mosque, Istanbul

Green into Blue, Mottled Whites

with apologies to Wikipedia
Sultan Ahmed Mosque

The sultan's decree remains
but tiles aren't cheap
The glazes have dulled.

The faithful donate carpets.
Gold and gems in the chandeliers
have been pillaged for museums.

The large iron chain was hung low
so the sultan, bowing his head,
would know humility.

Space was tessellated.
The one God, said the Pope on a visit.
I feel loved and understood.

Most of these colored windows
replaced by modern versions.
His feet were bare.

The Church of the Holy Sepulchre, Jerusalem

The Holy Sepulchre /
דער הייליקער קבֿר / הקבר הקדוש

בײַם גאָרטן־קבֿר
וואַרטן די פֿאַרשטויסענע געטער.
ווער ס׳איז מחייה־
ווער סע שטייט אויף תּחיית־
ווער עס קלײַבט צונויף מיט פֿײַער־צוואַנגען די מתים.

די געטלעכקייטן זוכן באַגריפֿן
וואָס זאָלן זיי אַרומנעמען,
ווי אַ בוים־חלל די זיסע־פֿלאַמעדיקע האָרנבינען.

At the garden tomb
the rejected gods are waiting
to resurrect, to rise from, to accumulate
the dead.
The godheads are looking for ideas
to embrace them
like sweet bees
seek the hollow in an old tree.

The Dome of the Rock, Jerusalem

The Dome of the Rock

An imitation church
on a venerated fragment of retaining wall
amuses the schismatic godlets
who aren't confused.

Blue dome above all
fire core below
this gold and stone
this bulging-creviced wall
its shawls and straining straps:

Knights all of us
of a glorious failing kingdom
clanking to conquer holiness
in part or whole
under our fluttering, notional standards.

The Chora Church, Istanbul

The Chora Church

Its name is translated as
the Church of the Savior in the Fields
but this, they say, is wrong.
Chora is an open space. The Land
of the Living: Chora Ton Zonton,
Jesus also given that name.
An openness to encompass all life.
Life busts out and over
like a child with a Crayola
colored red for blood, white
for albumin, pearly-gray for cortex
outside any lines, off the page
onto the ground. Onto a field.
The field surrounding us.
All forms of life cheerily burbling
hunting and sexing each other
swishing their molecules
in a reactive forcefield.
I understand now the rich feeling
of complete aperture
being given over to a savior
though I do not deify
Jesus. The translation is correct.

Tomb of Sultan Ahmed I, Istanbul

The Tomb of Sultan Ahmed I

The Clock Designer Reposes in the Garden of Sultan Ahmed I

Limbs of the clock organ scattered on the grounds.
Bars of the harem with space enough to glance.
Chill coins pressed in his sweaty English palm.
They presented maidens. Bodies nubile, faces prim.
He instructed every servant on the music and its time.
He discussed with the birds how he might sojourn
    with them.
The hour strikes. Elizabeth Regina takes a step.
Yes, she is an idol. And he is her adept.

James Turrell's "Spaces that Sees" at the Israel Museum, Jerusalem

Zackary Sholem Berger

Israel Museum

There is a cross in the temple of art.
Venerate the images others love
others' gods
so that your own may not be dragged
into the grime of spite, the sewer
of tselochis.

Church of the Holy Sepulchre, Jerusalem

Zackary Sholem Berger

Jesus Pantocrator

looks down from the firmament.
I could believe in a human savior
when not enjoined against it by an abscondent God.
Forgive me, clan of sapiens.
You are my favorite pantocrators
creators of the deity prescribed by Voltaire
that raving hater.

The Süleymaniye Mosque, Istanbul

Zackary Sholem Berger

Suleyman's Palace

The Light of Day

They used the jail to print books, or the other way
    around.
In either case the prisoners would be redeemed
by distant judges, face to the wall in a corner
till regime change
when they could be open, spine to the world.

Topkapi Palace Harem, Istanbul

The Harem

Seeing the changed face of the Black Chief
she knew she would not have empire.
She imagined herself a Ruthenian icon
in a cloud of incense.
Dying revered in a small town
a procession passing shutters.

Terra Sancta Church, 'Akko

> *There is no incarnation without a place.*
> — *Franciscan website*

Locked in a room outside of time
all flawed spiritdrunk people
launch polyglot harangue in deic jive.
They are trying to impale souls on minarets, shuls and
    steeples.
A cycle of forced conversions.

Let us bless and curse them.

Souls smash souls, casting fragments of hatelove.
Particles of religious mayhem.
This is the supercollider designed by gods above.

Gimel. Scrabbling for Shards

Lag B'omer

Like a record
Thirty-third
(And a third)

Counting days
In reveries
The needle stays

We know the groove
As we revolve
In annotated
Travelogue

I wake up with a craving for the whole damn diamond

yet scrabble for shards.

Light shatters on my grayish rainment.

Every hour is my friend:
I name them after beetles.

Elul

As a leaf, recollecting the calendar,
Remembers to drift,
Curses and verses (script of the new year)
Quiver and shift

As if the machzor on the shelf is moving—
Or slowly opens
Its pages to dusty reproving.
Which we ignore, often.

We strike selves like a crooked machine.
Ungainly parts.
Who knows if this location is open.
Or services hearts.

Selichos

Remembering skipped davening,
Awe flickers off, then on, near evening.

Arthropedic alefbeis
Between the clouds in graylit space.

Supplicants at open door
We join hands. Mornings, now, are for

Jokes, met with delighted honk
Or lifted eyebrow; bemused blink.

Abnegation Day

May the crimson turn to white (an easy fast)
And may we realize what (in recent past)
we should have done better (or resolved).
This won't be fast or easy (but surely sealed).

Daled. The Ladder Inside You

Translations

My Father Used to Call It Chatzos

H. Leivick

Midnight. My father called it Chatzos.
I greatly envy him that ritual.
Each letter of that text pursues me, as
He lamented Shechina's exile.

I suppose I'm doing much the same thing.
I mourn destruction and the guiltless dead,
I clench my teeth in the same grimace.
Missing: just his beard — a flaming red.

His fiery beard is gone away
But without a beard I'm no happier.
The midnight cry connecting him and me
Emerges now, in light of childhood years.

And my sons, in another fifty years —
Will they miss me with the same yearning?
Will they also jump from bed with a pious terror
At night, remembering a few verses of mine?

If so, hear my prayer, Lord of Time,
And show my sons some little mercy:
Wipe off, erase, like chalk from a board
These anguished nights of mine, in nineteen-forty.

At thirty

Abraham Sutzkever

At thirty my father's heart gave out
While playing Reb Levi Yitskhok's melody
On a small fiddle at nightfall —
The fiddle trembled childlike on his shoulder.
And its language, a bright magnet,
Drew the distant world
Into the shadowy hut
Where I, a seven-year-old dreamer,
Wrapped myself around
Fatherly knees.

It was — was — in bright Siberia.
A spot of sun, or the hot tongue
Of the freezing wolf,
Licked the snows on the pane
And couldn't melt through.
The only light came
From the fragmented sounds
Of the fiddle, sparking in stripes
Against my humid eye.
Suddenly my pale father
Grabbed his heart, jerked, wobbled
With his arm stretched out,
And into my arms his body fell
Together with the fiddle,
As a heavy branch falls

Onto a green wave
And is carried away....

Overhead floated a melody.
Down below, on the floor,
My father's last breath was failing.
And whether I'm convincing myself it's true
Or what I say is true:
Lying now eternally joined to a cold silence,
His lips confided in me:
"Thus, my child,
Test the weight of life in your arms
So you become accustomed
To carry it completely, to the end..."

Then the poet was born in me.
A kernel slumbered within me
Carrying in its core a certain mission.
I imagined I became the lord
Of forests, people, things.
Whatever I saw
Was my embodied desire.
My father's last will
Followed me from then on:
"Thus, my child,
Test the weight of life on your arms
So you become accustomed
To carry it completely, to the end..."
Now, when I have run up against my father's age,
Hurried up upon it,
And there's no way back or forward,

When I notice my face in a mirror,
My distant father
Wells out to me from its waves.
Perhaps I'm him, and my years
Are only a link to his departed life?
The same face as his,
Recollecting snow on windowpanes...
The same heart
Which is getting ready to give out,
And just like my father
I also own a little red fiddle:
See, I tear open my veins
And play on them my melody!

But there's no one here
Whose knees to wrap around,
Weighing out my life,
Dragging on, as with a wind,
My cloud of yearning to a clear destination,
Where all words come to rest,
Where days come together
But never meet.

I clasp in my fist, like a stone,
These thirty years
And hurl them into the cold
Mirror's chasm.

From Diary Poems

Avrom Sutzkever

Of course, your ladder's inside you. In-you is your
    ladder.
Not that ladder, anyhow, leaning out there on the attic.
The first climber is actually behind the second
Who is the first to the top — instead of the first.
A cloud darkens your pupils: a pointless reflection.
Words with six wings are ready for your rungs.
You wrestle with one, who touches your thigh.
You will always limp, climbing on the rungs.
Limp then. But don't neglect completion's line.
Your ladder won't fall down from quaking earth.
At night there are no stars, just the burning leaves of
    books.
There is none other. You are second, and the third.
In you, a living breath in a valley of bones.
No one enlivens them except for your breath.
In you, the weeping storm, the air of sea
that comes after it. The fecund kernel.
The triumph of the tree that comes tomorrow.

Explain it? Explain it how?
The sun didn't turn colder,
but she won't melt tears
and only childhood gets no older.

Youth, her brother, was trampled
like red grapes in the cellar.
The shadow's hair turns silver
and only childhood gets no older.

Her snows and her violets
are not to be had for gold.
Her king grows old, as does his kingdom
and only childhood gets no older.

from "Russia"

Dovid Hofshteyn

There on night's blue snows
among the bare tree-riders
my angel paces, guardian
of the first and silent rows

Under the high hot sky
neath faraways sunlit and wide
my wanton youth is gliding
in a frame of golden rye

Snows and breadths and heavens clear
My first, my purest memoriams to you!

Herring Barrels

Dvoyre Fogel

Round like the world, like the city
five hooped barrels of herring
in the grocer's
at 22 BROAD STREET.
Five round wooden barrels
of fat gray salted herring.
50 GROSCHEN EACH
JOSHUA SCHIMMELS
FAT HERRING
50 GROSCHEN EACH
And on faraway glassy seas
narrow ships loaded with fish
— fish gray and velvety like an autumn sky —
ships cool, blue, the faraway
of resigned steely landscapes
And on hot seas
of blue cobalt and ultramarine
ships loaded with oranges
meaty bananas and humid dates
Ships from brass landscapes
where the sun is a great metal ingot
where on streets elastic like gold foil
everything is for the first time and urgent.
Fantastic and out of nothing
like old world-weary bananas. Like oranges.
Like people who've gambled away their constellations.

I Prefer

Beyle Schaechter-Gottesman

I prefer
Narrow bent alleys
Knotty blue secrets
Dignified in modesty
Weighed down with intimations
Like the newly poor
Who don't beg

I prefer them
To bright boulevards
Gagging on their charm
Reaching to heavens
But never rising
Nothing real or deep

I prefer
Tender longing
For my old homes
Dark gates
Crooked sidewalks
Familiar stones
Seared into imagination
Silent doors shut
Tormenting me
Through the night
Not clear
Who or what
I long for

I Won't Ask

Beyle Schaechter-Gottesman

I won't ask
what I should
when I should

Though at night
I choke in stabbing pains

the dull word
just as well polished

I won't assault the waves in their depths
I won't let myself be
driven on by unloosed forces

I'll only look, and thread-thin
fall silent
I'll smile in blue just because
and overself, over them
be mute.

The eye speaks crystal clear wordlessly
And the unspoken word speaks,
talked about.

My Pedigree

Moyshe Nadir

My great-great-great grandpa
would crack heads
like people crack coconuts:
hang them around his neck
to keep track of a gnawed bone
or a woman torn open
and throw an arrow at his own eye in the water.

My great-great grandpa
polished pyramids.
He and his little brother
used to drag a pyramid
from Dignuz to Kardima
(by the waters of Cheftzar)
and then they would wipe their sweat
with big leaves
then these same leaves
would be savories
to eat with raw grass
and frogs.

My great grandpa
was a chunky high priest.
He used to stand there in his priestly garments
grinding pigeon shit and galbanum
together with urine
and say "Grind it up,
Grind it up"
(because the voice is good for the incense)

and yell at the Israelites
"Why are the lamb kidneys so dinky?
And why aren't you forgetting any stalks in the field?
And keep it down, because the incense
can't take in my sweet and holy voice!"

My grandpa
My grandpa was a kosher slaughterer
who ran his cleaver
over calves' necks
like a klezmer, maybe, with his bow
over the fiddle strings.
He'd mumble all sorts of blessings
which fell on his wet beard —
and get greasy from blood.
And God would lap it all up.

My father
was a well-put-together guy
in satin and silk.
Walked with small steps on Shabbos
(and in my mom's heart).
And when he was really pumped up
from good business and good liquor
and flushed from woods and wind
(and lust for young shiksas)
he'd grab his beautiful beard
between his hands
and say to my young mother:
Hey, I don't get no respect!
Reb Yoyl's son Zimele — he's my ancestor!

And sit down dipping pieces of cake
in a shotglass green with whiskey.

Me Myself
I wear colored ties
and clothes of the best wool fabric.
Got the best bed-and-table-manners
and women love my sass,
love my gray hat which sits rakishly
on my young gray head.
My love affairs are small and thought out.
They get worn out and boring, like the ties.
And I say often to my best woman in the highest
    moments:
"Like an undershirt, next to my own body,
I want to change my wife" — she is terrified by my
    crazy rudeness
and squeezes me even harder
hanging on my lips — on my heart
which is really beating, literally, on her lips.

And I'm good for ear and eye. My dilapidation
is like the sweet perfumed fading
of the last apple in the winter forest.
My soul often walks around without winter
    underwear,
without shame, but with pain
from people who profess shame
from pretend embarrassment
which dangles from their mouths
like the earrings of a woman who says No but does

Yes.
My eye is a sad brown. My ear is handsome.
The back of my neck is a bourgeois pretty-ugly.
My appetites frequently get eaten up
with the food I'm eating.
My weakness is: a fat Donhill pipe.
And a black wife — a little lightened up.
Like coffee with a splash of milk.
And a jug of sweet-sour white wine.
My coat is bright and wide
and covers up lots and often.
My pocket handkerchief understands
what's stolen by the corners of the eyes.
My nose is long — and knows the smell
of a hundred dollars or more.
It has its own concept of women and love.
To it, the whole world of Art is insignificant
compared to the tuft of hair
in my lover's underarm.

Some Guys

Avrom Reisen

Some girls go to dive bars
Others to cathedral
One guy likes a brothel
Another loves the shteebl

Believing is required
Everyone needs something
Whether it's the devil
Or someone in Heaven

What if you've got no one
and are just a hater?
You'll wander then like Cain
In every thoroughfare

Everyone will scorn you
Mock you and make merry.
And the whole world'll
Be your cemetery.

The Shadow

Natan Alterman

Once there was a man and his shadow.
One night the shadow stood up
took the man's shoes and coat,
put them on. Passing by
it took the man's hat from the hook,
trying as well to remove his head —
without success. It took his face off
and put that on too. If that weren't enough
next morning he went out with his walking stick.
The man ran down the street after him
shrieking to his friends: What a terrible thing!
It's a shadow! A clown! It's not me! I'll
write the authorities! He can't get away with it! He
　　wailed
bitterly, but little by little got used to it, fell silent, till
　　at last
he forgot about the incident.

Dream Diary (excerpt)

Bei Dao

After the outrages' autumn
November made stupid by frost,
Shadows in numerous layers
Flat against the wall.
A petrifying skeleton.
When you didn't return in time
the pit in my throat
turned into warm stone.
My suspicious behavior:
this season's military parade
rattles my windows.
People living inside a swinging bell.
With a running heart
I overlooked time.
You don't need to turn around.
A year in the midst of darkness.

Zackary Sholem Berger

All the Holes Line Up

Heih. Willing a Rhyme
Closing

I stay up late

Willing a rhyme with light
My mouth half-open.
I sleep too late.
With sun I'll rise buoyant.

Arguments: excuses.

Excuses that are castles. Collapsing forests
and aggressively honking fowl.
Notes fall off staves
into a boiling lake.
Jump:
clouds ripple an answer-no-answer.
String: the frame of options
we are permitted to carry in.
Don't touch till you are ready to help.

Some Time

The forms of things become
our wishes for them
in words we remember
from some time ago
when the world was hot and young

Intermomentum

Between moment
and moment
shadow
of a silence
echo of a roar
when no more
can be done
but stretch out hands
catch the spray

About the Translated Poets

Natan Alterman was a poet, translator, playwright, and critic. His work is considered part of the modern canon of the State of Israel.

Bei Dao is the pen name of Zhao Zhenkai. One of China's most important contemporary poets, he was exiled from China in 1989 due to his perceived involvement in the Tiananmen protests.

Dvoyre Fogel: A philosopher, art critic, and essayist, she wrote poetry and prose poetry in Polish (a language she was born into) and Yiddish (which she started writing in as an adult). She achieved some renown as the correspondent and collaborator of the Polish avant-garde writer Bruno Schultz. She was shot in 1942.

Dovid Hofshteyn was a Yiddish poet, a modernist, who managed to pair his careful neoclassical work with the political requirements of socialist realism. He fell victim to Soviet repression with the murdered poets of 1952.

H. Leivick was a poet of Messianic hope and tragic suffering who plumbed these topics to their painful depths. His verse drama The Golem was his best known work.

Moyshe Nadir was the pen name of Yitzkhok Rayz. He was a satirist, erotic poet, playwright, and critic, a committed Communist until he left the party and its publications in the wake of the Molotov-Ribbentropp Pact.

Avrom Reisen (1897-1953) was a prolific poet, short-story writer and journalist. His minimalist, realist verse was touching, evocative, and socially conscious without oversentimentalism.

Beyle Schaechter-Gottesman was a children's author, poet, and songwriter. Many of her songs are part of the contemporary Yiddish art song repertoire. Her poetic work, by contrast, is darker and more brooding.

Avrom Sutzkever's poetry was lyric and apolitical; he saw himself as a modern prophet. During the Holocaust he was a partisan fighter of Vilna and saved Jewish cultural treasures; after the war in Israel he founded the 20th century's most important Yiddish journal.

Glossary

davening = [Jewish] prayer (Yid: davnen)
shteebl = small prayer house (Yid: shtibl)
tselochis = spite

About the Author

Zackary Sholem Berger is a poet, translator, and short-story writer working in Yiddish and English. His writing has appeared widely. Currently he is a regular contributor to the *Yiddish Forward* and lives in Baltimore with his wife and children.

In his parallel professional life, he is a primary care doctor who tries to help patients achieve what they want for themselves as individuals, in their community, and in society. He has published two books about patient-centered care, *Talking to Your Doctor* and *Making Sense of Medicine*, and is working on a book about how doctors and patients can share in decision making. Berger is also the treasurer of the political action committee Clinicians for Progressive Care.

He can be followed on Twitter as @ZackBergerMDPhD. His web site is zackarysholemberger.com.

www.ingramcontent.com/pod-product-compliance
Lightning Source LLC
LaVergne TN
LVHW041343080426
835512LV00006B/600